Giggles, Gags and Groaners

RIDICULOUS RIDDLES

WRITTEN BY:

STUART A. KALLEN

Published by Abdo & Daughters, 6535 Cecelia Circle, Edina, Minnesota 55439.

Library bound edition distributed by Rockbottom Books, Pentagon Tower, P.O. Box 36036, Minneapolis, Minnesota 55435.

Cover Illustration: Terry Boles
Inside Illustrations: Terry Boles

Edited by: Rosemary Wallner

LIBRARY OF CONGRESS CATALOGING-IN-PUBLICATION DATA

Kallen, Stuart A., 1955-
     Ridiculous Riddles/written by Stuart A. Kallen
         p. cm.--(Giggles, Gags and Groaners)
     Summary: A collection of riddles including "What is a cats favorite dessert? Mice cream!" and "Why did the baker stop making donuts? Because he just got tired of the hole business!"
     ISBN 1-56239-126-7
     1. Riddles, Juvenile. 2. Wit and humor [1. Riddles.
     2.Jokes.] I. Title. II. Series: Kallen, Stuart A., 1955-
Giggles, Gags and Groaners.
PN6371.5.K36 1992
818' .5402--dc20   92-14772
                                   CIP
                                   AC

Table of Contents

Critter Crack-Ups 4

Monster Moans 15

Spaced Out! 22

Food Fiasco 26

Moans and Groans 31

CRITTER CRACK-UPS

What do you call dinosaur car crashes?

Tyrannosaurus wrecks!

How do you make dog bread?

Out of collie-flour!

What do Eskimo swine live in?

Pigloos!

Why did the dinosaur wear tennies?

Because nineys were too small!

What is a cat's favorite dessert?

Mice cream!

Why couldn't the cow give milk?

Because she was an udder failure!

Why did the horse become a priest?

Because he wanted to be put out to pastor!

Why did the chicken jog across the road?

Because she needed more eggsercise!

Who was president of the jungle?

Ape Lincoln!

Who is a duck's favorite president?

Mallard Fillmore!

Who is a pig's favorite scientist?

Albert Swinestein!

What is a dog's favorite state?

Barkansas!

What is a black widow's favorite drink?

Apple Spider!

Why can't leopards hide?

Because they are always spotted!

What happened when the mosquito bit the movie star?

She became itch and famous!

Why didn't the fish hear the boat coming?

Because they were hard of herring!

Why did the fish orchestra sound so bad?

Because they needed a piano tuna!

How can pigs fall in love?

Because beauty is in the sty of the beholder!

Why is a horse like a cannibal?

Because he eats his fodder!

What are the largest ants in the world?

Eleph-ants!

How do you fix a broken gorilla?

With a monkey wrench!

What's black and white and black and white and black and white?

A penguin falling down the stairs!

Why wasn't the frog in the choir?

Because he croaked!

Why can't you trust the fastest leopard?

Because it's a cheetah!

Why did the pigeons form an orchestra?

Because birds of a feather Bach together!

Why does a grizzly have fur?

If he didn't he would be a bare bear!

Why did the girl brush the bunny?

Because she needed to comb her hare!

Why couldn't the elephant fly?

Because the airline lost his trunk!

What do you get when you cross a cow with a duck?

Milk and quackers!

How do ducks send phone messages?

They use a quacks machine!

What is a cat's favorite book?

Tail of Two Kitties!

MONSTER MOANS

What did the vampire say after he bit the man?

"Fangs a lot!"

Who did the witch call when she needed to fly?

Broom service!

Why did they build a fence around the graveyard?

Because people were dying to get in!

Where does Dracula keep his money?

In a blood bank!

What instrument did the skeleton play?

The trom-bone!

How did the vampire know he was catching a cold?

He started coffin!

Why did Frankenstein like flowers?

Because he *rose* from the dead!

Why did the witch go to school?

So she could learn to spell!

Who is a ghost's favorite president?

Franklin Boo-sevelt!

Where did the cyclops want to live?

Eye-daho!

Where did the cowboy ghost live?

Moan-tana!

Why couldn't the vampire play baseball?

Because he lost his bat!

Where do they make werewolf movies?

Howly-wood!

Where did the vampire buy his clothes?

Cape Cod!

What is a ghost's favorite food?

Ghoulash!

What is a mummy's favorite music?

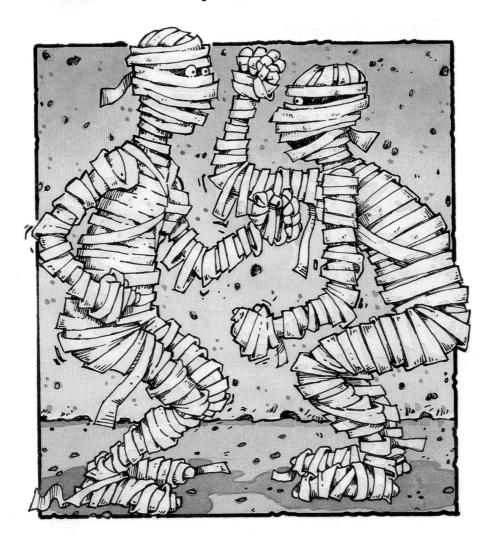

Wrap music!

Where did the vampire swim?

In the blood stream!

What are the gravediggers favorite candy flavors?

Straw-bury, ras-bury, and cran-bury!

What did the witch say when she went to the party?

"What the hex going on?"

What was Dr. Jekyll's favorite game?

Hyde and go shriek!

What Navy protects spook ships?

The Ghost Guard!

What was the Swamp Creature's favorite food?

Marsh-mallows!

What's the first thing a ghost does when he gets in a car?

Fastens his sheet belt!

What do sea monsters eat?

Fish and ships!

SPACED OUT!

Why was there a shower of moonlight?

Because the moon was waning!

Why couldn't the library buy more books about fairy tales?

They ran out of elf space!

Why is the man in the moon so tired?

Because he's out all night!

Why is the moon bald?

Because it's 'airless!

Why are there so many books about Mars?

Because it's the read planet!

What is an astronaut's favorite music?

Rocket Roll!

Why is the moon worth one dollar?

Because it has four quarters!

What did the planets say after a visit to the dentist?

"Look, Ma, no gravities!"

What did the girl make her new kite out of?

Flypaper!

FOOD FIASCO

Why didn't the drummer finish his salad?

Because he skipped a beet!

Why did the fruit trees get married?

Because they made a nice pear!

Why could the farmer hear so well?

Because he ate many ears of corn!

What did the grape say when it was stepped on?

Nothing, it just gave a little wine!

What do you get when you cross a potato with a flower?

A rose-spud!

What government official is in charge of meat?

The Secretary of Steak!

Why were the grapes in trouble?

The got themselves into a jam!

What do you call a pie with eggs, broccoli, cheese, and poison?

The quiche of death!

Why did the woman turn the stove over?

Because she wanted to make upside-down cake!

Why did the police come to the party of the dried grapes?

Because they were raisin a ruckus!

What did the coconut say to the almond?

"Let's go on a date!"

Why did the baker stop making donuts?

Because he got tired of the hole business!

What did the salad oil say to the refrigerator?

"Shut the door, I'm dressing!"

MOANS AND GROANS

Why did the clocks jump off the wall at the party?

Because time flies when you're having fun!

Why did the hungry man go to the beach?

Because of the sand which is there!

When is a car not a car?

When it's turning into a driveway!

What did the dandelion say to the lawn mower?

"Take me to your weeder!"

Why did the farmer buy new pants?

He liked the overall effect!

How can you tell when it's going to rain?

The clouds put on their thunderwear!

What did one angel say to the other?

"Halo there!"